Mapping the Seaside

Written by **Jen Green**

Illustrated by **Sarah Horne**

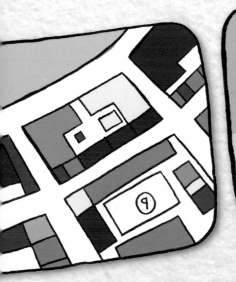

First published in 2015 by Wayland
Copyright © Wayland 2015

Wayland
338 Euston Road
London NW1 3BH

Wayland Australia
Level 17/207 Kent Street
Sydney, NSW 2000

Series editor: Victoria Brooker
Editor: Carron Brown
Designer: Krina Patel

A CIP catalogue record for this book is available
from the British Library. Dewey number: 526-dc23

ISBN: 978 0 7502 8577 3
Ebook: 978 0 7502 9119 4

Printed in China

1 3 5 7 9 10 8 6 4 2

Picture acknowledgements: Cover: top centre REX/Geoff Moore,
bottom centre MicaTravel1/Alamy. Pages: 4 Geoff Moore/REX; 6 MicaTravel1/Alamy;
10 Chris Ison/Shutterstock; 17 Adam Woolfitt/Robert Harding/REX; 18 Skyscan.co.uk/J Farmer;
20 Skyscan.co.uk; 26 moodboard/Alamy.

The website addresses (URLs) included in this book were valid at the time
of going to press. However, it is possible that contents or addresses may
change following the publication of this book. No responsibility for any
such changes can be accepted by either the author or the Publisher.

Wayland, part of Hachette Children's Group
and published by Hodder and Stoughton Limited
www.hachette.co.uk

Contents

BY THE SEASIDE

The seaside is the border zone where the dry land meets the ocean. Towns and villages along the coast allow people to make use of the sea, and also enjoy the seaside.

Maps help you to enjoy places like the seaside too.

What are maps?

Maps are drawings of the landscape seen from above. Imagine you are a seagull, soaring over a seaside town. This bird's-eye view is the same as a map. The landscape looks very different from directly above.

This photo shows Lulworth Cove on England's south coast.

This is a map of the same cove.

Side view

Overhead view

TRY THIS!

To read and make maps you have to learn to see things from high in the air, like a bird. Compare these two drawings of a seaside funfair, from the side and from directly overhead. The familiar shapes of slides and roundabouts are hard to recognise from directly above.

PLACES TO VISIT

Many seaside towns have tourist maps, which show all the best places to visit. Top attractions such as a pier or lighthouse are shown in little pictures, so they are easy to recognise on the map and in real life.

Finding the way

Tourist maps can be used to find your way and plan a route around the town. The bird's-eye view shows whether the places you want to visit are far apart, or next door to one another.

You can tell whether you need to turn left, right, or go straight on to get from one place to another.

Tourist maps help you find the way without getting lost.

TRY THIS!

Look at the map below. Plan your route from the Arcade to the Sealife Centre. Write down the directions to follow if you don't have a copy of the map.

Sights of Sea Town

The title of the map explains what the map shows.

SEASIDE SYMBOLS

Tourist maps have little drawings of key sights such as the pier. But most maps don't have room for detailed drawings or labels. Instead, they use special signs called symbols.

Symbols make the map less cluttered, so it is easy to read.

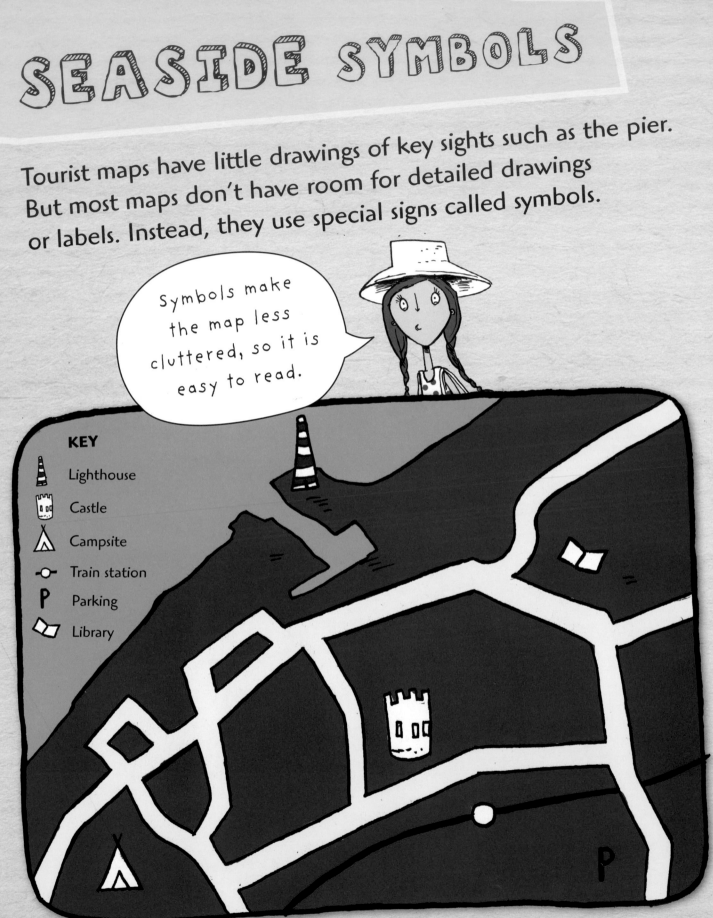

KEY

Lighthouse

Castle

Campsite

Train station

Parking

Library

Types of symbols

Four types of symbols are used on maps such as this map opposite. Symbols include letters, such as P for Parking. Lines of different colours are used to show roads and railways. Coloured shapes show places such as parks. There are also very simple pictures, such as a little tent, which means a campsite.

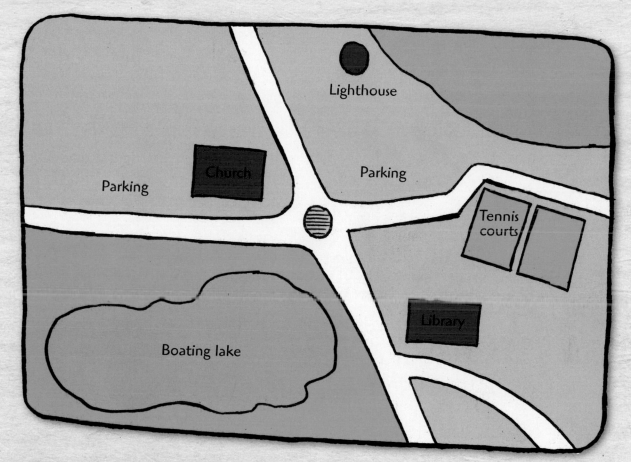

TRY THIS!

The map shown above has labels instead of symbols. Trace the map and use symbols instead of words. Use the symbols shown on this page, or make up your own.

DIRECTIONS ON THE BEACH

If you stand on a beach and look straight out to sea, you are facing in a particular direction. North, south, east and west are the four main compass directions.

The red magnetic needle on a compass always points to north.

You can use an actual compass to find out which way you are facing.

Using compass directions

Sailors out to sea use a map and compass to find their way across the open ocean. Compass directions are shown on most maps. North is usually at the top, and south is at the bottom.

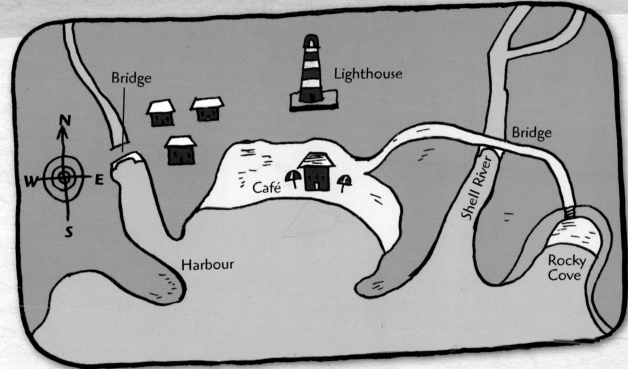

TRY THIS!

Compass directions can be used to locate places on a map in relation to one another. For example, on the map above, the lighthouse is north of the café. Look at the map and answer these questions.

- Which features are north of the harbour?
- In which direction would you walk to get from the café to Rocky Cove?

A HARBOUR TO DIFFERENT SCALES

All maps show the landscape much smaller than it really is. That way, the map fits on a piece of paper that you can hold in your hands. All maps are drawn to a particular size. This is called the scale.

The scale bar at the side explains the scale. For example, I centimetre on the map may stand for I kilometre on the ground.

Harbour

P

0   0.1   0.2   0.3   0.4   0.5   km

This small-scale map shows a whole town with harbour.

Large or small?

Some maps show a small area such as a harbour. Others show a town, or even the whole country. The scale of the map affects how much detail you can see. Imagine you are a seagull, flying high in the sky. You can see a large area but not much detail. If you swoop lower, you can only see a smaller area, but details such as buildings become clear.

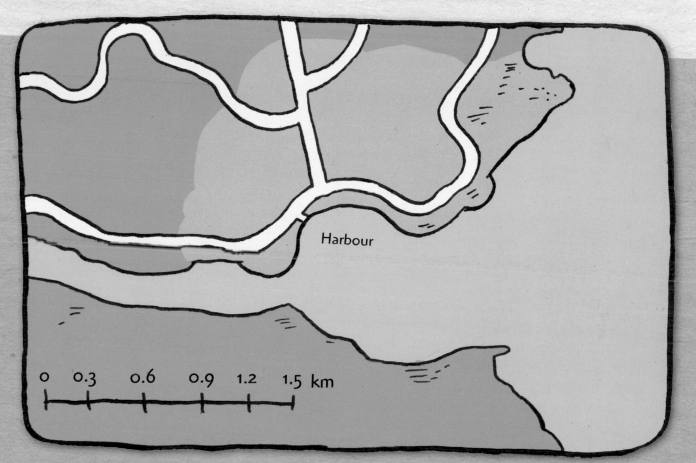

Harbour

0   0.3   0.6   0.9   1.2   1.5 km

This large-scale map shows part of the town (the harbour) in more detail.

TRY THIS!

Maps on the Internet have a zoom feature that changes the scale of the map. Practise zooming in and out of a map on the Internet.

PLAN OF A PIER

Many seaside towns have a pier or sealife centre. Maps called plans show the inside of buildings like these. Architects draw plans when they design the building. Everything is measured very carefully.

That way, the builders know exactly where to put walls, windows and doors.

KEY

☕ Café

🍦 Ice cream

🛍 Shop

🐟 Fishing club

♫ Bandstand

Using plans

Plan maps can be used to find your way around a building, just as ordinary maps are used to explore outdoors. Seaside attractions such as piers and sealife centres often display a map, so visitors can locate the rooms or areas they want to see.

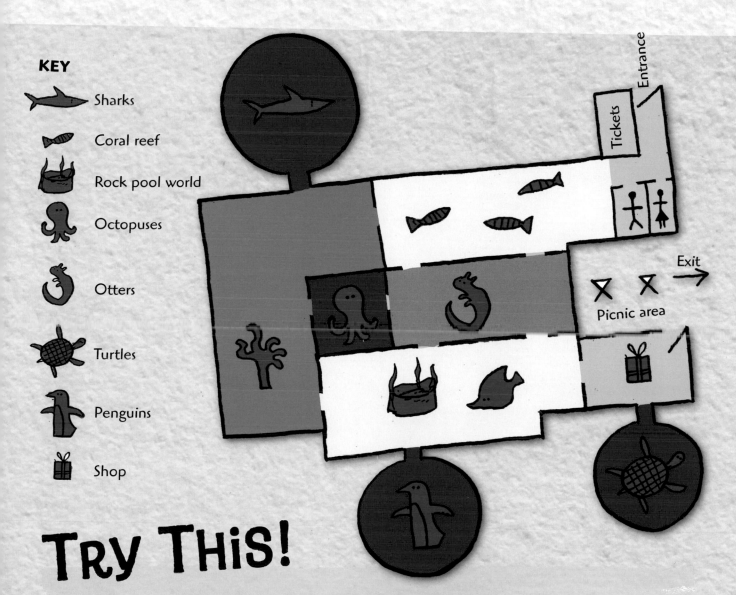

KEY

Sharks
Coral reef
Rock pool world
Octopuses
Otters
Turtles
Penguins
Shop

Entrance
Tickets
Exit
Picnic area

TRY THiS!

The plan map above shows a sealife centre. Use the map to plan your visit. You want to see the sharks, otters, octopuses and penguins. Which way would you go?

CAMPSITE IN A GRID

The map below shows a campsite by the sea. Maps like this one are divided into squares. The squares are made of lines running across and up and down the page. The squares form a grid, which you can use to locate places on the map exactly.

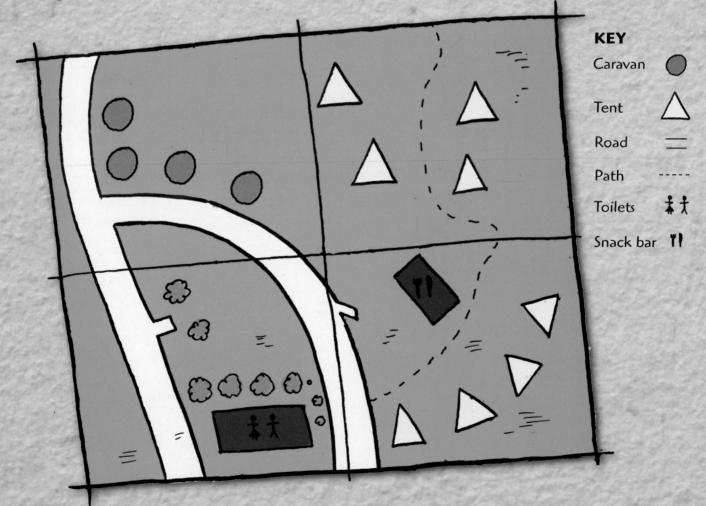

KEY

Caravan ●

Tent △

Road =

Path - - - -

Toilets 🚻

Snack bar 🍴

Grid references

Look closely, and you will see that the lines across the map have letters. The lines running up the map have numbers. The letters and numbers come together to pinpoint exact locations. This is called a grid reference. For example, the toilets on the campsite are in square A2. Grid references are always read in a certain order. Start at the bottom left-hand corner. Run your finger along the line, and then up the map, to find a location such as square C2.

TRY THIS!

Look at the map and answer these questions. Which squares are the tents in? Name a feature shown in square A2.

WALK AT THE RIVER MOUTH

River mouths are places where rivers meet the sea. These areas may have mudflats and marshes. There may be cliffs or sand dunes. You will also find bridges and breakwaters.

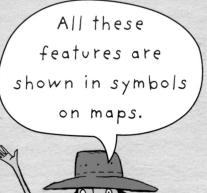

All these features are shown in symbols on maps.

Walk with a map

To use a map on a river walk, you need to know which way you are facing. Hold the map out and turn around until what you see on the map matches the features in front of you. Or, if you have a compass, you could turn around until north on the red compass needle points in the same direction as north on the map. Then off you go!

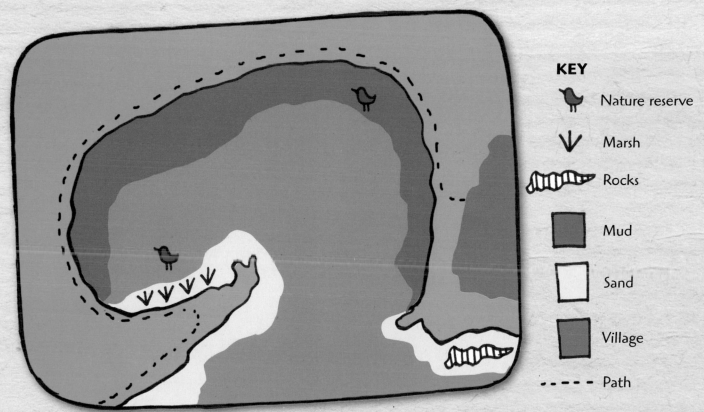

KEY

🐦 Nature reserve

𝖵 Marsh

〜 Rocks

▪ Mud

▫ Sand

▪ Village

- - - - Path

The key explains the new symbols.

TRY THIS!

Look at the map and the key. Describe the features you would see on a walk from the village to the sea.

ON THE CLIFFS

Many places by the sea are far from flat. The land may slope gently down to the beach or port, or cliffs may tower over a harbour. But how can you show these hilly places on the flat surface of a map?

Contour lines

Lines called contour lines show cliffs, hills and valleys on maps. These faint lines join places at the same height above sea level. Little numbers on the lines show the height of the land. The numbers always face uphill, so you know which way the land is sloping.

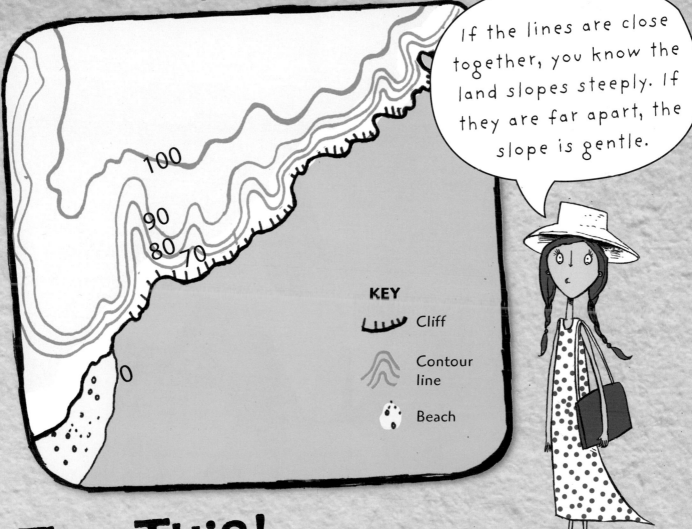

If the lines are close together, you know the land slopes steeply. If they are far apart, the slope is gentle.

KEY

Cliff

Contour line

Beach

TRY THIS!

Study the map above. Look at the contour lines. What is the height of the cliff? Where are the highest and lowest points? Can you tell how the land rises and falls?

SEASIDE WEATHER

Not all maps show the natural features of a landscape. Some give different kinds of information. For example, weather maps show what the weather will be like over the next few days.

Weather maps help you plan your day at the seaside — you will probably want to be outside on the beach if it is sunny, but inside if it is raining.

SUNDAY

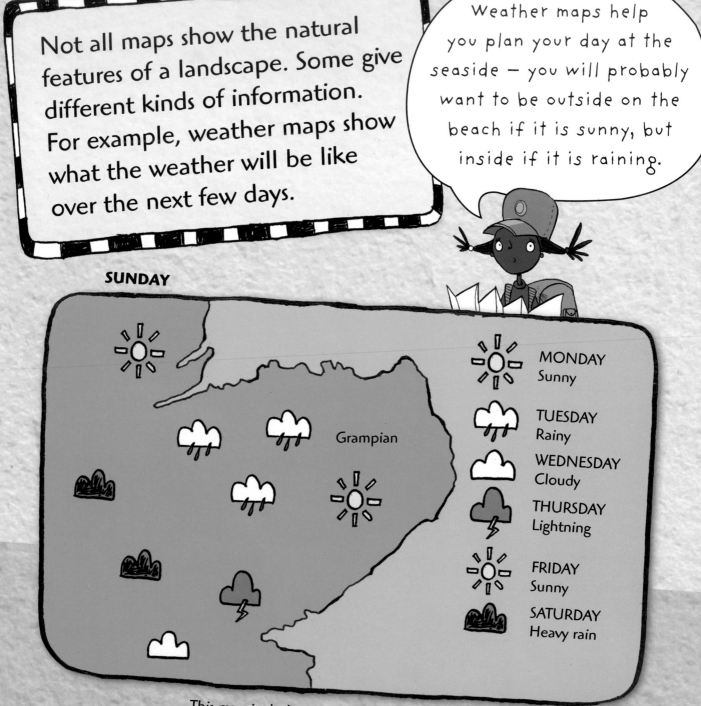

MONDAY
Sunny

TUESDAY
Rainy

WEDNESDAY
Cloudy

THURSDAY
Lightning

FRIDAY
Sunny

SATURDAY
Heavy rain

Grampian

This map includes a seven-day weather forecast of the Grampian region, in Scotland.

Weather symbols

Weather maps have special symbols that show weather conditions, such as sunshine, rain, clouds and thunderstorms. As on other maps, the key shows the meaning of the symbols. Some weather maps show other kinds of information, for example, the yearly rainfall, or temperatures at different times of year.

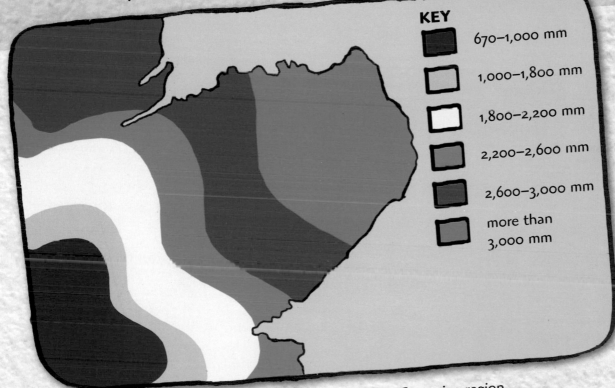

KEY

670–1,000 mm

1,000–1,800 mm

1,800–2,200 mm

2,200–2,600 mm

2,600–3,000 mm

more than 3,000 mm

This map shows yearly rainfall in the Grampian region.

Try This!

Make your own chart to record the weather for a week. You could do this either at home or on holiday at the seaside. Use the weather symbols shown on this page.

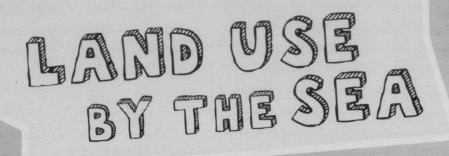

LAND USE BY THE SEA

Some maps give information about how the land is used, or the activities that go on there. Called land use maps, these maps tell you about people as well as places.

Land use maps may show a whole town, or just one building, with rooms that are used in different ways.

Seaview

Shore Street

Main Street

Ocean Drive

Harbour Hill

P

KEY

Hotel

Public building

House

Café

Shop

Office

P Parking

What goes on where?

Land use maps use different colours to explain how the land is used. For example, on a town map, houses may be shown in one colour. Workplaces such as docks, factories and offices are shown in a different colour. Places of interest, shops, car parks and green spaces appear in other colours. These maps make it very easy to see what goes on where.

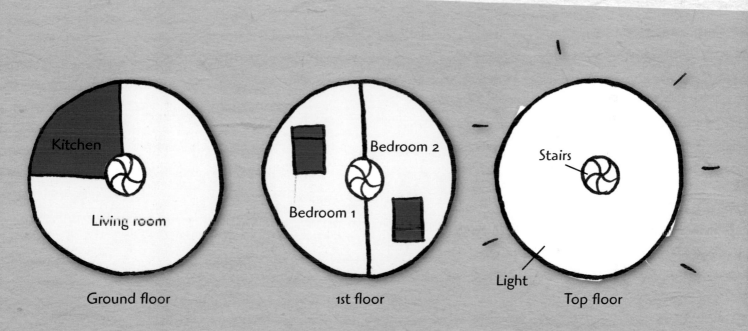

Ground floor   1st floor   Top floor

This land use map shows the rooms in a lighthouse. There are several floors.

Try This!

Look at the map of of the town opposite and answer these questions. Where are most hotels found? What is the main shopping street?

ARRIVING AT THE SEASIDE

Have you been to the seaside? If so, how did you get there? Many people come by car. Drivers use special maps, called road maps, to find their way on journeys.

Many motorists use a book of maps, called an atlas. A long journey will take you over several pages of maps.

Road maps

Road maps don't show the landscape in detail. Towns and villages are shown as dots or coloured shapes. Motorways, highways and small roads are shown as lines of different colours.

Railways

Many road maps also show railway lines. The map does not show the line in detail. Only the stops are marked, so people know where to get on and off.

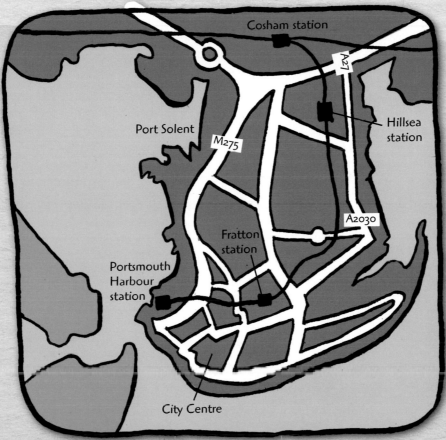

This map of Portsmouth shows main roads and the railway line.

TRY THIS!

Look at the map of Portsmouth and answer these questions. You are at Port Solent:

- What is the quickest way to reach Portsmouth city centre by car?
- How many stops are there on the railway between Cosham and Portsmouth Harbour?

ON THE ISLAND

Islands are special places completely surrounded by water. Some islands can be reached by a bridge or tunnel, but many can only be reached by sea or air. Ferries carry people from the mainland to the island.

KEY

Ferry route - - -

Port ●

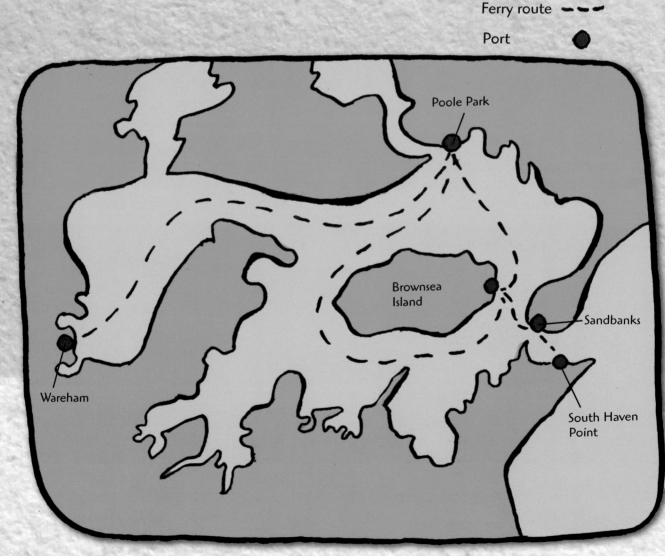

This map shows the ferry routes to Brownsea Island.

Treasure maps

In days gone by, pirates sometimes buried treasure on remote islands. They usually made a map to show where treasure was buried. Or they might give directions, but not show the hidden location.

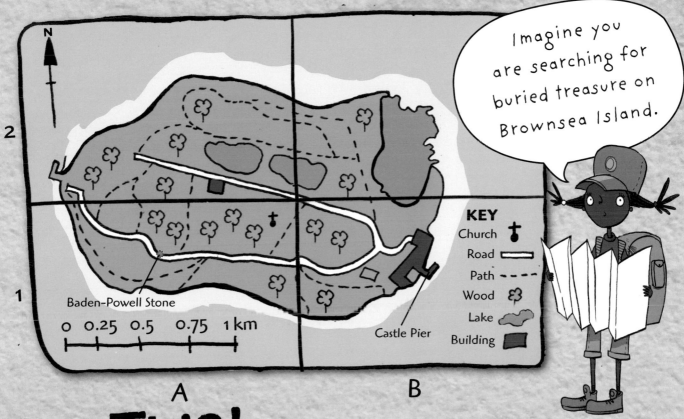

Imagine you are searching for buried treasure on Brownsea Island.

KEY
Church †
Road ▭
Path - - -
Wood ✿
Lake ～
Building ▬

Baden–Powell Stone

0   0.25   0.5   0.75   1 km

Castle Pier

A   B

TRY THIS!

Follow these directions, then answer the questions. Land at Castle Pier. Take the road past the hide and turn right at the church. Walk west for more than a kilometre. Turn left soon after you pass a building on your left, then first left again. The treasure is buried in front of the monument on your left. Where is the treasure buried? Give the square.

What the words mean

Architect A person who designs buildings.

Breakwater A wall built to protect the beach or harbour from powerful waves.

Compass A tool that shows directions and helps you find your way.

Contour lines Lines on a map that show the height above sea level.

Grid Lines running across and down a map that divide the map into squares.

Grid reference Directions for a location provided by the grid on a map.

Land use map Map that shows what land or buildings are used for.

Location Place.

Key Panel on a map that shows the meaning of symbols.

Mudflat A flat area by a river mouth that is covered by mud.

Plan A large-scale map that shows the inside of a building.

Road map A small-scale map that shows roads.

Scale The size a map is drawn to.

Street map A large-scale map showing the names of streets.

Symbol A picture that stands for something else.

More information

Books

Marta Segal Block and Daniel R Block, *Reading Maps* (Heinemann, 2008)

Jack Gillet and Meg Gillet, *Maps and Mapping Skills: Introducing Maps* (Wayland, 2014)

Sally Hewitt, *Project Geography: Maps* (Franklin Watts, 2013)

Claire Llewellyn, *Ways Into Geography: Using Maps* (Franklin Watts, 2012)

Websites
BBC – Landscapes

www.bbc.co.uk/scotland/education/sysm/landscapes/
Explore the landscapes of Scotland and develop your map skills.

BBC Schools – Weather

www.bbc.co.uk/schools/whatisweather/
Learn about weather maps and how weather affects people.

KIdsGeo.com – Geography for kids

www.kidsgeo.com/geography-for-kids/
Learn about the Earth and geography skills.

Mapskills (PowerPoint) – Think Geography

www.thinkgeography.org.uk/Year%20 8%20Geog/.../Mapskills.ppt
This site explains map skills and has lots of exercises to practise your map skills.

Ordnance Survey – Map reading made easy

http://mapzone.ordnancesurvey.co.uk/mapzone/PagesHomeworkHelp/docs/easypeasy.pdf
Download this handy guide to map reading.

Index

Titles in the series:

9780750285742

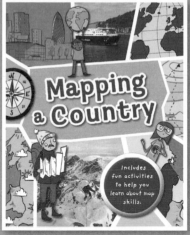

9780750285735

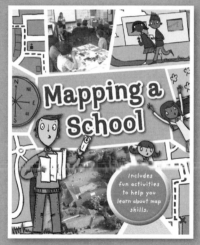

9780750285780

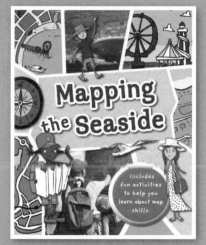

9780750285773

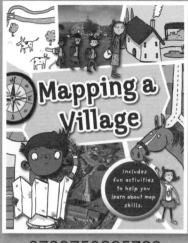

9780750285728

9780750285766